Itinerary

- Paris, France
- London, England
- St. Petersburg, Russia
- Bruges, Belgium
- Warsaw, Poland
- Tallinn, Estonia
- Oslo, Norway
- Prague, Czech Republic
- Geneva, Switzerland
- Amsterdam, Netherlands
- Palma de Mallorca, Spain

Tour Europe in Fashion

Sandy Mahony
Mary Lou Brown

A Coloring Book
& More!

Paris, France

Paris, France

CAFE

MENU
~ ~ ~~ — 7,5
~ · ~ — 29,0
~ · ~ — 130,0

Paris, France

Paris, France

Paris, France

Paris, France

London, England

St. Petersburg, Russia

St. Petersburg, Russia

Bruges, Belgium

Bruges, Belgium

Warsaw, Poland

Tallinn, Estonia

Oslo, Norway

Prague, Czech Republic

Prague, Czech Republic

Geneva, Switzerland

Amsterdam, Netherlands

Amsterdam, Netherlands

Amsterdam, Netherlands

Palma de Mallorca

adventurelearningpress.com